Contents

INTRODUCTION

By the Conference Chairman, Mr Ric Foot

Hardly a month goes by without some new aspect of information technology emerging, as one might perhaps expect from what is estimated to be the world's fastest growing industry. It is becoming difficult even for those who are engaged in I T on a day to day basis to keep up to date with developments.

So when a group of us from Aslib, the Institute of Information Scientists and the Library Association met in July 1982, it was agreed to organise jointly a seminar to give news of at least some of the more important developments now taking place or being planned.

We were fortunate to obtain as speakers some of the best authorities in these new fields and the result was the 'I T's on Screen' Seminar held on Monday November 8th 1982 at the Polytechnic of the South Bank. Suitably, of course, 1982 was Information Technology Year.

The papers which follow have been prepared specially by the speakers for this publication and cover:

Telesoftware - a means of transmitting computer programs by means of the broadcast teletext services and linked by the BBC to their computer literacy programmes.

Cable - heralded by many to be potentially the most far-reaching development due to take place since the growth of the railway systems in the last century. Some of the major issues are discussed.

LaserVision - the video disc system developed by Philips can add a new dimension to education and training, and become a major new communication and marketing tool.

Teletext - the broadcast text on screen service which has become certainly the fastest growing evidence of I T for residential consumers.

Viewdata - the long-awaited growth of viewdata is now in evidence. For consumers, the realities of teleshopping and telebanking and other interactive and informational services are here now, and major new initiatives based on the Prestel public system are discussed. For business use, both public and private systems are growing rapidly. A specific private case study is presented.

On behalf of my colleagues from Aslib, the Institute of Information Scientists and the Library Association, I wish to express our thanks to all our speakers and not least to Mr John Butcher MP Parliamentary Under Secretary of State for Industry who so kindly agreed to open the Proceedings for us on November 8th. Our gratitude and thanks too to Rob Palmer, the Conferences Officer of the Library Association, who did a magnificent job of organising us all. Without all these and the kindness of the South Bank Polytechnic, the Seminar would not have taken place.

I am sure the best appreciation of the speakers and organisers would want is that you find these papers interesting and useful, and that you will enjoy reading them.

KEYNOTE ADDRESS

John Butcher

First of all, thank you very much for the opportunity to come along here this morning to kick off the proceedings at what, as Ric Foot has just described, is a unique occasion.

It really does bring back old times for me, because in a previous incarnation I happened to be Chairman of the Further Education Committee in, I think, the third largest education authority in the country. I remember wrestling with the vagaries of 'pooled' expenditure and the politics (with a small 'p') of polytechnics for many years. I hasten to add that I had an awful lot of interest and a lot of fun during that period of time.

I would like to add my compliments to those of many others for the initiatives that have been taken at this polytechnic, the Polytechnic of the South Bank. Here the academic implications and the practical implications of information technology are well and truly on board.

I was interested in Dr Beishon's mention of his Department of Bakery, for you will know that there is an awful lot of bakery going on in the Department of Industry at the moment; a lot of Kenneth Bakery.

'Information Technology' is a comparatively new phrase but the technology of information will be a theme all too familiar to many of you here today. Those who deal with the dissemination of information, particularly through the library service, whether they are in, attached to or outside the official education sector, have been in the business of information provision, messaging and retrieval for many decades. It is true to say that Aslib has been in information management since 1924.

I think it was Joe Stalin who first coined the phrase that information is power. He used the information at his disposal to awesome effect in order to achieve power within a certain structure. Perhaps in our context today, we should postulate the theory that information is enlightenment, information is the freeing of the individual and of groups of individuals from certain restraints.

Within the education service, there have been many developments. I believe that in this forum it is right that we should reaffirm and, indeed, begin to discuss some of the new ways in which information can be disseminated and, dare I say, paid for. I am not trying to work against the traditions of the free library service as it was originally invoked, or indeed, to suggest that one should make profits from the dissemination of information, but I hope that you would agree with me that we are involved now in some very controversial areas, particularly in the area of copyright.

Whereas authors of the written word feel that they have a
pretty raw deal when it comes to the proper recompense for the
volume and ratio in which their works are read, we may also find
that, more and more, we will come up against a similar problem
with regard to the information which is disseminated via computer
terminals from main frame computers. We know that there is a
controversy at the moment on the copyright of video cassettes.
There is also a growing controversy over the way in which the
authors of software should be rewarded for their talents.

The danger is that cassettes and diskettes can be duplicated
very easily and therefore produce a loss of revenue for those
who've put in the hours of ingenuity in order to take a particular
program to market. This I'm sure, is one of the areas you will
be able to examine today, either under the Telesoftware or indeed,
under the Cable heading.

I was interested to hear that already at this Polytechnic,
they are pursuing ideas of knowledge-based systems. Intelligent
knowledge-based systems is a key area of the Alvey Report. I hope
that we shall use Alvey and the four major areas that Alvey is
asking us to study, together with the breakthrough in cable technology and the liberalisation programme in telecommunications, to
produce an explosion of information, to produce the widest possible
and cheapest available distribution of information to a very wide
public.

I note that you are going to be talking about Telesoftware
and I would like to put it to you that we should not get hamstrung
by terminology at this early stage in the debate. 'Telesoftware'
can be applied to two quite distinct methods of disseminating
software. The first method is the transmission of software literally
through the ether, as a broadcasting service, as almost a sub-
routine of Teletext; that in my view is Telesoftware in its purest
sense.

The second aspect, which already concerns a number of you,
is the dissemination of software and programmed information
through the telephone network, through Modems into such things as
Viewdata and Prestel. Now that again is another area of very great
dynamism, and one which your service, I think, could do very much
to add to.

I hope that we will be able to solve the problems of the
dissemination of that information. That is, as I said earlier,
the question of the proper reward for the authors of that information.
Now, it may may be that John Radcliffe or Frank Hall will tell you
about something called Dongle plus encryption**now there's a lovely
term. As I understand it, that means that in the not-too-distant
future, we shall be able to introduce 'smart' Modems which will
prevent the duplication of information which has been transmitted
either through the air or along television lines or along telephone
lines. These will prevent the duplication of that information into
intermediate storage and the subsequent dumping on to disc and then
its duplication for use, free, by others. If we can crack that

problem, using the technology which we hope will shortly be available to us, that will give us a breakthough in permitting authors of various programs, various books if you like, whether they are electronic or whatever, to receive the proper reward for their efforts.

I hope that in the United Kingdom, we can take a lead, not just in this service, but in all areas of information technology. I mentioned Alvey. I have great faith in Alvey. I think that if we pursue it vigorously, then we can have our Fifth Generation Computer and add to that the freeing of the UK information distribution network.

By that I mean not just the liberalisation of British Telecom, but the introduction of Value Added Network Services in a regime that is the most liberal in the world, and I say that advisedly. I think you can see that we have an opportunity here to take a world lead.

I hope that within the UK you can continue to set up databases, to use DP techniques, to use the opportunities of cable and viewdata and telesoftware to add to the services that you already provide. If this is done in a proper way, it may well give us a dominant position in the international markets.

We can do what we've always done well. That is to say to the English-speaking world, not only is there a mine of information in literature and technology in the United Kingdom, but we have now knocked it into shape in terms of the electronic media to allow you to purchase it, to place it through your education system and get the widest possible audience for this wealth of information at a price and regime that is less arduous. For example, if we were to sell information into Nigeria, using the techniques that are now available, the Nigerian educationalists can use these systems to get to a much wider audience much more quickly with a much better supervisory function from the centre. I put it to you that the technology is simply expanding the impact which the systems that you have implemented have already had. It is simply a matter of scale, of getting the message over to a much larger group of people.

Looking at information technology, in its general context, I would put to you the following proposition: the proposition is based on two alternative views of the year 2000.

In the year 2000, we can either have a nation in which the products of information technology have not been applied and one in which they have. Let's assume that they had not been applied. It would be true to say that it would be a nation with large numbers of people involved in unpleasant, repetitive and possibly dirty and antisocial tasks. We'd be a nation of low-paid people, a nation in which there was constant acrimony between the various groups in our society, and if I may say so, between politicians. There would be haggling over scarce resources which would cause,

I think, a very unenlightened position within the United Kingdom.

Now contrast that with a society which has made proper use of information technology. It should be a high-wage, high-productivity economy; it would be a nation in which the thoroughly unpleasant and antisocial types of work have been more or less abolished. It would be a nation which is producing surplus wealth and a nation which can afford the proper environment, the enlightened environment, a proper social wage, a nation in which political acrimony is being reduced, and a nation which, above all, is better informed.

Now I hope that the achievement of the better-informed society is very much central to your objectives today. We are not here simply to talk about technology for its own sake, we are talking about making information and its application available to an ever widening audience. And if the technology allows us to do that more cheaply, and more conveniently and more pointedly (I'm sure that you'll come to 'narrow-casting', incidentally, on cable), then surely we can evolve a happy alliance with that objective in mind.

If I understand the theme of your conference correctly, then that is what it's all about. All I'm asking is that you continue to do what you've always done well, which is simply that you use the technology to do it on a much greater scale. So I wish you the very best in this particular conference and I can assure you that we shall look very closely at your deliberations when they've been minuted and when they come into the Department of Industry, and it may well be that there will be an occasion in the not-too-distant future when we can follow through the initiatives you may have launched this morning.

** A 'Dongle' is a computer hardware tool which is supplied with one particular program and is then attached to the back of the customer's computer. Since only the right dongle will respond to a particular command in the software, thereby enabling the rest of the program to be run, it provides some kind of protection for the copyright software. It is no good copying the software if you can't use it for lack of the hardware. - Ed.

TELESOFTWARE AS PART OF THE KNOWLEDGE NETWORK

John Radcliffe

As the Minister has said, this mysterious expression 'Telesoftware' means essentially the provision of computer programs or data by broadcast or land line in a form in which they can be received directly into the memory of a computer. It is that direct link straight into memory that is, I suggest, the revolutionary aspect of telesoftware.

Now, there is, as some of you will know, a certain amount of telesoftware already available on Viewdata and there has been a broadcast telesoftware experiment conducted by Brighton Polytechnic in collaboration with the BBC and the IBA. Now, as part of our Computer Literacy Project, the BBC is going to provide a national service of telesoftware from January on an experimental basis. We have got test transmissions going out at the moment. As far as we know, this is a 'world first' for this country, and a very remarkable new development. This is very much an experiment and we'll be trying to respond to the way people react to it; the responses of users will be very important to us.

This has been part of the Computer Literacy Project which I've been running for the past couple of years, which includes television programmes, books, correspondence courses, referral and information systems and computer hardware and software. I'd like if I may, to spend just a minute of two setting the context of our telesoftware service within that Computer Literacy provision because I think our experience has thrown up a lot of ideas which will be of great interest to many of you here.

When we started making programmes about computing and information technology, we addressed ourselves to the questions which were very much in people's minds at the end of 1979 - early 1980, and they were essentially to do with the social impact of computers: What effect will this technology have on my job, on my office, on my classroom, on my company and on my industry? and so on. We made a number of programmes about these issues and we found that whenever you make programmes about information technology, you get a very positive public response, more positive than you get on most technical subjects. But also something else happened. People started to ask us other questions, which were much more nitty-gritty questions about the technology.

They were questions like: 'What is a computer? What is a 'Memory'? What is a computer language? How does a computer process data? What is a databank? What do you mean by word processing? How do I control a computer? (perhaps the most important question of all)'. It was these questions coming in to us from many quarters that led us to the idea, about two and a half years ago, of this Computer Literacy Project which we've been developing.

We decided to commit large resources to this. A television series is a very expensive beast. We wanted to find out what the audience actually wanted, and in the process, we discovered some very interesting things which surprised us. First of all, we found that the interest in this technology did not just extend to the committed, to the computer-literate, to the people who buy the magazines, or to teachers or businessmen who are going to have to use the technology. We found that it extended down into lower socio-economic groups, it extended to women as well as many men, and it extended right up the age range from teenagers right up to people in their sixties and seventies. People didn't just want in a general way to be told about the technology, they actually wanted to learn about it. Furthermore, they had a greater propensity to learn about this subject that any other subject that we've researched. And at the same time, of course, hardware was getting cheaper; suddenly it was getting within the reach of many people. The third thing we found, though, was that people were very anxious about the technology, not so much about the effect of it but about their capacity to understand it. Because of the extraordinary way that we have brainwashed ourselves in the past, there appear to be a few people who see themselves as able to understand technical subjects, a lot more people who would like to be able to understand about them but think of themselves as disqualified and alienated, but yet with this propensity to learn.

Interestingly enough, there was an age element to this. Each age cohort thought that the age cohort below them would be better at the subject. The thirty year olds thought that the twenty year olds would do better; forty year olds thought that they were getting past it but the thirty year olds would do better and so on; the twenty year olds were terrified of the teenagers.

Now that clearly is a myth, but it was a dangerous and powerful and pervasive myth and one with which we would have to deal. Of course it's nonsense - our brain cells don't die off that fast and when we get older, we know how to use the ones that are left rather better, I hope. But this was the myth, a powerful myth in people's minds. So we set out to make a television series to deal with that myth, to convince large numbers of people, all those people going up the age range, and down the socio-economic range, of many different backgrounds with many different motives, that information technology is an accessible subject, a fascinating subject to anyone who is prepared to make the effort to understand it. You might say that we set out to provide a gateway into the subject.

Now we have transmitted our television series three times in the early part of this year and we're putting it out again now, twice, and as Ric Foot has said, as many as seven million people saw one or other of the programmes. We did manage, through making the series very friendly and accessible to reach a lot of people who, I think, would have defined themselves as computer-illiterate. Over fifty per cent of the audience were over thirty five, 25% of the audience were over forty five, significantly, and 46% of the audience were women.

This in itself was interesting, but even more interesting was this, because this was only part of a large, many-sided project in which we collaborated with many institutions. We produced a book, for example, The Computer Book, which is now being published in the United States. BBC Publications said to me: 'What do you think ought to be the print order?' I said 'Well, fifteen thousand'. We sold sixty thousand in twelve weeks. The National Extension College produced a correspondence course, Thirty Hour Basic. They said to me 'What do you think ought to be the print order?' 'Ten thousand,' I said. They've sold a hundred thousand, a hundred thousand copies of a course of programming in Basic. We set up a Referral Information System on the subject; we have had 90,000 enquiries - it costs us a fortune to deal with them. Again, I could have guessed it would have been a third as many as that.

We developed the BBC Micro Computer. Now we made decisions about that about eighteen months ago. People said to me 'What should be the target number of machines that you will sell?' So I said 'I don't know, let's try 12,000.' That was a very bad mistake-Acorn have sold fifty thousand machines, despite the existence of many other machines, in the last year.

Now all of that is not a sign of our singular genius. It's a sign of something that is going on in this society, which is extremely interesting and significant. It's the sign of a tremendous demand for information about this technology, a genuine desire to learn about it and a willingness to get involved with it. When you read the popular press, you read many stories which have to do with people's fear of the technology. You sometimes get the impression that people are somewhat Luddite about the technology - not so. The British people appear to us, on the strength of an awful lot of research and investigation, to be responding in a very positive way to this technology and they want to get their hands on it, and they want to know more about it.

There may be an explosion of information, as the Minister has said, but there also seems to be an explosion of interest in knowing more about this subject. We have ridden in on that wave and we are continuing to ride it, with some discomfort, I may say, because it's going very fast. I suggest that we're moving much more quickly than anyone could have anticipated to a situation in which a computer will be as common an item in the home as the stereo system. That's going to happen much more quickly than we could have imagined two years ago.

I think the significant point to stress at this Conference, which is not very commonly realised in the population yet, is that we are not talking about a communications device. This is where telesoftware is particularly significant. We're talking about making the home computer into the home information terminal. We're talking about the intelligent television receiver. We're talking about a way of giving more people in their homes access to more information than has ever been the case in human history.

Now, many, many people are buying micro computers now, faster
and faster and many of those micro computers have got communications capabilities and more will have in future, both Viewdata
and broadcast Teletext. But as we all know, as anyone knows who
is involved in this business, the great need now, in fact the
obstacle to forward progress, is in the field of the software,
not the hardware. The hardware has developed to a point wherein
if all further development stopped now, it would take us ten years
to exploit the possibilities in the way of hardware that already
exist. But the software, the applications programs, which ultimately depend on thinking, creative imput, imagination in devis-
ing ways in which we can use these extraordinary machines, of good
software there is a fearful shortage. It's as if the record player
had been invented but there weren't nearly enough good discs to
play on it, or indeed, there wasn't nearly enough musical talent
to even record on discs. And it is significant (this is another
factor that we've discovered) that people's motives for acquiring
this hardware are quite strongly educational, people buy them for
schools to use them for educational purposes, people buy them for
their kids to use them for educational purposes - they want their
kids to understand about the technology and feel that this is the
technology of the future, they don't mind their kids playing Pac-
man or Breakout or whatever, as long as they can also do something
worthwhile: the educational possibilities are immense and revolutionary but by no means fully exploited. Indeed, they're at the
very beginning of development, because we've got to find out how
to use the equipment, we've got to bring together the educationalists and the people who know about computers in order to devise
good software that works.

It's taken us 20/25 years to learn how to make a reasonably
good educational television. I would hope that it would take us
a lot less to learn how to develop good educational applications
programs because we haven't got that long. But there is this
very great shortage of software.

Now, many people are trying to fill this gap. BBC Publications
and many other educational publishers are publishing applications
programmes. There are many commercial providers. There are bodies
like the MEP (Micro Electronics Education Programme) of the DES.
Many people are trying to get good educational software published.

But the problem is to identify and push it round the system, so
that lots of people have got access to it. And this is where telesoftware comes in, because you can distribute by cassettes, you have
to record it on to a cassettes and then you have to write some accom-
panying literature, and you have to put it into a packet and you
package it (very often the packaging will cost more than the cassette)
and then you have to mail it to somebody, or you have to put it into
a shop and they have to come in and buy it. The same thing applies
to a disc. If you send programs out as listings, it's a long, cumbersome process to actually take those and put them into a machine.
It can be done, but it's not a very elegant process.

We realised fairly early on in developing our project that the

combination of broadcast Teletext with the BBC Micro Computer
created the possibility of a broadcast telesoftware service.
And we insisted that there should be a telesoftware capability
built into the system from the outset. We had the great advantage of having access to a national Ceefax system, and David
Wilson will be telling you about that Ceefax system in the session
this afternoon. But we realised that if you put those two ideas
together, the computer and the Ceefax system, it would be the
basis of a new communications system.

And, in a nutshell, we have had this machine developed, an
add-on addition to the BBC Micro Computer, this little white box
here, which is a receiver that can receive broadcast teletext
signals but can also recognise coding on those signals which can
then be fed into the microcomputer; this enables the microcomputer
to recognise that as a computer program and load it into memory -
a very elegant and simple system.

You need the microcomputer, you need a way of displaying the
information from the computer, a VDU, (it doesn't have to be a
television set) and you need the receiver which you simply connect
up to the aerial - and you're in business.

I am going to give a short recorded demonstration. The first
of these is a very simple word recognition programme for primary
schools. It is meant to recognise which of the words on the left,
when they have an 'e' added to them, make another word. There is
a tremendous amount of motivation given to children if they can
learn through an interactive process. What we did was to select
a particular page of Teletext on which if you had an ordinary
Teletext set, you would have seen a listing with some extra bits
of coding. The ordinary user of a Teletext set would be able,
if he had the time and energy to actually lift that out, to do so,
but the owner of a special receiver can take it into his memory.
Now, he's got the program , he can use it, modify it and then,
of course, store it.

My point is simply that one can treat the broadcast signal,
or, indeed, the Viewdata signal as a source like any other source.
You can use a cassette filing system; if you want to take material
on a disc, you use the disc filing system; here, you simply go to
the Teletext filing system. And when we've got the service fully
in operation, you should have the choice of about twelve programmes
at any given time. We will be circulating them around from early
in 1983 and they will be receivable by anybody who has that particular add-on extra to a BBC machine.

Now there are some intrinsic limitations, or rather significant limitations that do exist on broadcast Teletext. One of them
of course is space - you can't occupy huge swathes of Teletext pages
because they are needed for other things. We are going to confine
ourselves initially to programs up to about 8 K and many of them
will be smaller than that. Don't forget also that if programs
require documentation, we're going to have to send out documentation
by post, because we can't necessarily assume that people can receive

that documentation and record it on printers. They will be able to eventually.

Also, of course, because we have not yet come to terms with the possibilities of encryption, at the moment we are saying to ourselves that we can't charge them anything, it's got to be a free service. It will be mainly serving the educational system, so we'lll be transmitting perhaps half or two thirds of our telesoftware to use in schools and colleges, although we're going to keep about a quarter or third for what we will call something like a Club Page. We will say to people: Send us your software and we will look at it, and if it appears to have merit, our Telesoftware Organiser will get it into shape fit for transmission, we'll ensure from the user that it doesn't actually belong to Texas Instruments or that he's not expecting us to pay him a heavy royalty for it, and we will transmit it. And the other thing we'll be doing is saying to users: Tell us if what we're giving you is any good or if you would like us to give you something else. In other words, it is an experimental service relying very heavily upon the feedback that we get from people over the first year of operation.

Of course, many of the limitations which I have mentioned for broadcast telesoftware don't exist nearly to the same extent when you are using a Viewdata system, and I must stress that there is going to be a Viewdata module rather like this one which will also give people access to many Viewdata systems; there is already being developed, I believe, a cheap acoustic coupler which will achieve something of the same result, and I suspect many of the same facilities are going to be available on many other machines before too long.

It's interesting, incidentally, just as a tailpiece before your questions to mark the speed at which people's thinking on this has advanced. In Australia, where they are also effectively developing a Telesoftware service, I said I would be very interested to see any telesoftware they had, and they said, ' Okay, we're delighted to give it to you, we'll send it over the line. We'll send it over the Viewdata link', and so it will be possible for a school to write a programme in New South Wales, for it to be sent over a line to us in London and we can transmit it via the BBC, all within a very short space of time.

What we have here is the beginning, just the beginning, the first, tentative beginning, of what is going to develop into a home information system which will be connected to cable systems, will be able to receive broadcast systems, will be able to receive direct broadcasts from satellite, will be able to take systems over the Post Office telephone lines, which, as I have said, is going to give more people more access to more information than they have ever had in the past.

CABLE

Frank Hall

I am very glad to have this opportunity to say something about
cable to this audience. A lot of the current publicity concen-
trates on entertainment, which is vital as I shall explain, but
in the longer term, it is the non-entertainment aspects which
are the most exciting.

But firstly, if I may, a bit of history. Unfortunately,
it is the usual British story: at an early stage, we led the
world in cable, but by a series of missed opportunities, we have
allowed that position to slip and today, there are many countries
particularly in North America, who have a much higher utilization
of cable.

Gloucester, 16 March 1951, saw the momentous occasion when
Link Sound & Vision Services Limited (now part of Visionhire
Cable) opened a cable television service, the first town-wide
system to operate in the UK and, we believe, worldwide.

That was the start of a decade of wiring expansion based
entirely on entertainment, of course. A large part of that
cable provided HF signals and had a four channel maximum capacity.

It is interesting to note that only today, some thirty
years later, do we have four channels generally available, so
our original investment decisions seem to have been justified.
We established a thriving industry but it could not survive.

What went wrong? Basically two things: firstly, succes-
sive governments encouraged both BBC and IBA to improve their
transmitting abilities, so that many of the pockets of poor
reception were eliminated, thus removing the need for cable
inputs. Secondly, in order to protect the BBC and ITV companies, the authorities refused to permit cable operators
to put out on their networks anything but their public service broadcast programmes. Indeed, for a long time, we were
not even permitted to put out on our systems the IBA programmes
receivable from an 'out of area' IBA transmitter.

For these reasons then, the cable operators found themselves with substantial investments in networks but a declining
usage. Pressure on Government to allow other uses for those
networks led to nothing but a few small experiments, and these
were so regulated that they could not succeed until the latest,
the pay pilot schemes currently being operated.

There was, however, one alleviation of the cable operators problems. Many local authorities, who in this country own some 40% of the total housing stock, grew concerned at the proliferation of aerials on rooftops and the cable operators had the opportunity of providing a bulk service, particularly on new housing developments. The local authority, as landlord, collected a slightly increased rent from the tenants and paid the cable operator to provide a signal imput to every home under long term contracts. What will our skylines look like when we have dish aerials for satellite reception as well?

Apart from these bulk schemes, you might wonder how it is that the cable operators have retained any subscribers at all. We have done it by providing a good service, and it is reasonably clear, I think, that people will pay a small sum to have a proper signal piped into their homes. There can be little doubt that they will pay rather greater sums to have additional channels. Just look at the video recorder explosion for evidence. Our continuation of old cable services is evidence of our long term committment to cable systems.

I have deliberately dwelt on the negative aspects to emphasize that regulation and protectionism are responsible for the British public today having a far smaller choice of programming available than most of North America and much of Europe.

My company recently published a series of articles entitled 'The Cable Revolution'.** I had hoped to be able to distribute copies today but the demand for the book has been so great that we have just run out of our first print. Some have in fact been distributed to all local authorities, and you may find a copy in your own organisations. At the back of the book, we have set out a comparison from which, I think, you will see the enormous difference between what happens in Manhattan, where they have a thirty-channel cable system, and what happens here.

The Manhattan choice at 9 p.m. on 7th June 1982 contained a large number of different channels including normal entertainment of the sort which we are accustomed to seeing here, but I would draw your attention to the fact that there is also: a documentary on black ghetto life; a documentary on American twentieth century history; a play in Spanish; cultural programmes including the ballet dancer, Nureyev; an educational channel; a seminar on the peace movement/nuclear arms; several plays; a Chinese cooking programme for the Chinese minority; plus a number of sports programmes and the CNN news channel - all available at the same time. And on our channels here, there were until recently three programmes; today there would be four. Our excellent public service broadcasters cannot possibly provide the range of programmes our diverse population wants.

You may not like everything that is scheduled. Do you like every newspaper and every magazine that is published? Do you like every picture that has been painted? Is what you like the same as

what your children like or what your parents like? There are
those who say such choice is bad for us, but who has the right
to decide what we should like and dislike? Is your dislike a
good reason to prevent people from having the choice? I suggest
that a wide degree of choice enables individual tastes to be far
better satisfied and will help with the ethnic minority problems
that many of our cities face.

Does this mean that cable will be seeking to provide thirty
channels of trash, of wall-to-wall Dallas or Coronation Street?
Any cable operator who does that will quickly learn better. No
home and certainly, no one person, can view a number of channels
simultaneously. A cable operator wants as varied a menu as
possible so that he provides something for as wide a spectrum
as possible, We are accustomed to talk of 'ratings' of forty
or 50% plus - but a cable system providing thirty channels would
be delighted to achieve an average rating of 3% for each channel.

And what of British content? Initially, until networks have
grown large enough to produce reasonably-sized audiences, we must
rely largely upon existing product. There is a vast library already in existence, both here and abroad. I know that using such
material will not bring added employment to those concerned with
making programmes, but I hope they will take the long term view.
When cable is established, the excellence of the British product
should surely enable it to survive and expand. The lack of
confidence in their own abilities being demonstrated by the
programme makers is, to me, one of the most surprising parts of
the cable debate.

I have dwelt to some extent on the entertainment that cable
will provide, mentioning in that context additional educational
types of programme. I should just mention now the technological
state of the art. Let me say I am only a simple cable operator,
certainly not an engineering boffin, and I am definitely not
going to talk about the Minister's 'Dongle plus encryption'.

You may know that in America, which has the most developed
cable operation, they use a copper coaxial system using a tree-
and-branch technology. Without boring you with too much technical
detail, let me just say that the tree-and-branch concept results
in every programme that is available at the system's head-end
also being available at each outlet point in the subscriber's
home. A new technology is being developed and we have reason to
believe that the UK is in the forefront, which is generally
described as the switch system. Under this arrangement, the input
to the home is limited by a small capacity cable which can provide
perhaps four channels at a time and the subscriber is able to call
up the particular channel that he wants to see by the use of a
simple pad, similar to the existing television set remote control
pads. The basis of this of course is that no one person can look
at more than one programme at a time and it is unlikely that any
one home would want to receive more than four programmes at any
one time in the future. If he did, then of course, an additional

cable could be run, but in general, we believe that three or four is likely to be the maximum for a very long period of time.

This technology has a number of advantages, although it is not yet fully developed and is certainly not yet proven. It could also work well with optical fibre and that is another area in which we have considerable expertise in the UK which we need to develop. So the Government seems to believe, and I would certainly agree, that the development of UK cable systems could lead to a substantial involvement with the most modern technology both in system design and in types of cable used.

So, what about our expectations now? With one important exception, we see the framework contained in the Hunt Committee Report as providing the environment in which cable can now develop and, we believe, develop fast.

The one exception is the length of the franchise. Hunt suggests ten years. Ten years initially is just not long enough security of tenure for the vast investment. I know that period relates to the operator and not the 'provider' of cable systems. But in my view, there can be no difference if private companies are to invest in cable. The separation in the terms outlined by the Report is like an investor putting up a block of shops with someone else being wholly responsible for choosing the tenants, that someone else having no interest in the financial health of the investor. Under those circumstances, how on earth does a cable provider negotiate a commercial deal with a new franchise holder?

The Hunt Report suggests the terms of cable franchises should be similar to the term of IBA licences. But no explanation or logic for that deduction is given. Indeed, if you look at the relationship between income and capital assets in the two types of business, you will see why it is so illogical.

I have mentioned thirty channels: the number may well of necessity vary from place to place. Some of the major conurbations should be able to support a larger number of channels than perhaps the smaller towns. Their needs are probably greater. There are, for example, a number of ethnic minorities in some parts of London and other cities, each of whom should be catered for by the new cable systems, and no doubt there are also in the larger conurbations a greater variety of specialist requirements, whether it be for educational or general interest in hobby-type activities. Only cable can provide the number of channels that are needed.

So much for the entertainment channels. I have dwelt on them at some length because unfortunately, there is no evidence that many people will pay, at this stage, for modern information technology systems. You only have to look at Prestel to see the problem. But we do now have the opportunity to lay down a modern cable system which will fulfill all the needs that we can foresee for the next twenty five years, which will be made viable by the requirements for entertainment, on the back of which - but only on the back of which - a national information technology service can be provided.

May I just emphasize this: whatever cable system is used, the cost of installing it is very high indeed. The better and more advanced the technology, the wider the range of services to be provided and the more expensive it will be.

Unfortunately, all the evidence shows that, for domestic purposes, the general public will not pay for information and does not yet understand data communications at home. This is the main reason why Prestel has not become a major domestic product.

On the other hand, people do expect to pay for home entertainment. Over the years millions have been spent on gramophone records, on audio tape, on hi-fi equipment, and today millions are being spent on video recorders and video tape.

The penetration rate for video recorders in the UK has surprised everyone: per head of population, we are second only to Japan and miles ahead of America with its better disposable income.

Many of us have come to believe that our public service broadcasting is the best in the world. Perhaps those who so assiduously spread that concept should just be a little less arrogant about their own product and ask themselves whether the large demand for pre-recorded video tape is not evidence that a large number of people want a greater choice.

To return to non-entertainment. Things that can be added very economically. What sort of things are we talking about? We hear statements like tele-shopping, tele-banking, security and so on.

Let me take a few examples. Tele-shopping can range from the simple presentation every day, perhaps with a teletext type service, of the current charges for the main provision lines in the local supermarkets or other providers of groceries, a form of advertising of course, but I would have thought a useful consumer device. You can move up from that to a presentation of fashion goods by picture, or of course of furniture or anything of that kind. The simple pressing of a button could ensure that the shopkeeper does something for you - either sends you a brochure, asks a salesman to call or, in some cases, you could actually order the goods. The advantages to mail order concerns are of course considerable.

Tele-banking could save us all a lot of hassle. There would be no need to go to the bank. You could perfectly well call up

your own statement. You could make instructions to the bank to
pay money from your account to the local authority for your rates
or whatever. You could amend your standing orders, and a large
number of banking services could be available to you at home at
the flick of a switch.

Many of us have electricity and gas meters in our homes.
Many of us find it inconvenient to be present when the meter
reader wishes to come, and this is a very expensive operation
on behalf of the electricity and gas undertakings. There is no
reason why electronically the state of each meter should not be
transmitted back to the undertaking body so that bills can be
calculated without the necessity for physically calling on and
reading each meter.

Those are some of the easy applications. For this audience
I should add that it would be equally easy for individuals at
home to have access to, and send messages to, local libraries,
both for the purposes of enquiring whether particular volumes
are available and making reservations as necessary, but also to
have access to a local information data base.

Which brings me to the flights of fancy which I believe are
not as far away as all that. Already in America they have interactive systems working which provide a number of these services.
They also provide means by which individuals can be polled, and
to quote a rather silly example, there is a film extolling the
virtues of these systems which shows the ending of a horror picture and before the film is finished, viewers are asked to vote
for 'Do you want a happy ending' or 'Do you want an unhappy ending?'
By pressing the appropriate button, the majority gets what it
wants. Now, as I say, that is rather a silly example, but I think
it indicates the extent to which you can go and the extent to which
you can obtain instant responses about various questions. The
ramifications need thinking about.

In this context, I should also mention security, whether it
be burglar alarm systems, fire alarms, or even 'panic buttons'.
In America they already have a number of cable systems offering
such security services, and I know of one town at least which has
been operating a security service for a number of months where
at least one life has been saved because, as a result of the
emergency call arrangement, the police and ambulance services
were available much more quickly than could otherwise have been
arranged. When you're the sole occupant of the house lying on
the floor with a gash in your head, you might crawl to an appropriate button but you might find it difficult to dial 999 and
answer the appropriate questions. That is exactly what happened
in the case I have mentioned.

Moving a little further ahead, we should then be able through
our cable systems to do a lot more work from home than we can at
present. We can have access to our company's data base and we can
send messages.

Over the weekend, there have been reports in the Press that the response from the public is likely to be less than enthusiastic and certain suggestions have been made about the level of charges. Far be it from me to refute the findings of very expensive research carried out by a highly respected organisation. Let me just say that it is very difficult to obtain an enthusiastic response about something which is so far beyond the majority's current perceptions.

The financial situation will <u>not</u> be easy. A cable franchise is no licence to print money. But unless we start, we shall never find out and we risk depriving ourselves of immense opportunities. They are there if we want to grasp them. I believe we shall.

** The Cable Revolution - Britain on the Brink of the Information Society Edited by Andrew Neil. Available on request from Visionhire Cable Ltd, Visionhire House, POBox 43, Station Way, Crawley, West Sussex RH10 1JA, subject to availability.

LASERVISION SYSTEMS

Paul Bradley

1. ## INTRODUCTION

    Information Technology, as we have already heard, has been
    with us for some time in one way or another. What the In-
    formation Technology Year has achieved is to expose the
    various technologies more vigorously to its potential end
    users. The Information Technology Year has concentrated their
    minds and created a lot more interest in the uses and applica-
    toins of new communication techniques.

    The technologies I want to talk about today are both new and
    old. I am going to talk about the interface of two very
    separate technologies which give some meaning to the saying
    that 'The whole is greater than the parts.'

2. ## IT'S ON THE SCREEN

    The Optical Video Disc system has recently been released in
    the UK as a consumer product. It offers the potential of very
    high quality pictures coupled with two discrete sound tracks
    that in the consumer market can be used for stereo sound.
    Other features are offered with this system but I want to talk
    to you about its applications outside the consumer market, its
    applications in industry and education.

    LaserVision, as this technology is called, is for the playback
    of pre-recorded material. It is not capable today of recording,
    as is the case with video cassette recorders.

3. ## THE OLD TECHNOLOGY

    The storage and dissemination of information from a central or
    remote data base via a linked communications line is the old
    technology I referred to earlier. There are new ways of per-
    forming the task but nevertheless, computers have been around
    as long as I have. In fact, I was born just ten months before
    the first electronic computer was put to use.

    Computers are able to display text and graphics but are unable
    to display pictures as stills or in movement sequences other
    than as line drawings.

    Therefore, for the storage of high quality pictures, black
    and white or colour, the computer has some inherent limitations.

4. ## THE NEW TECHNOLOGY

    The technology of optical video discs are not unlike audio discs

in their appearance, 12" in diameter, but they are coated
with a highly reflective surface in order that the information
they contain can be 'read'.

These discs contain a maximum of 55½ thousand tracks, each
track being only about 1½ microns apart. On each track (or
spiral, as in fact they are) can be stored one complete
video picture. The information density of an optical video
disc is therefore 55½ thousand   pictures per disc side.
It is possible to accurately access any of these individual
pictures as frames or sequence of frames, thus giving moving
pictures.

Maximum access time to any frame is in the order of three
seconds. This important feature is not available with video
tape or film but it is an essential facility when requiring
and designing interactive programmes.

The information on the video disc is protected by a tough
protective coating and it is therefore difficult to damage.
Additionally, no wear or tear to the disc occurs when the
information is 'read' because a very low output laser is
used as a 'pick-up' and only the light beam touches the disc
surface.

5. <u>BRINGING THE TECHNOLOGIES TOGETHER</u>

The question of what industry will do with these technologies
when linked together is being addressed today in Japan, USA
and now Europe.

Many organisations spend considerable sums of their hard-
gained profits on such things as corporate communications,
staff training and product merchandising. They strive to
achieve their objectives in the most cost-effective or econ-
omic way. Information Technology has meant that new ways of
communicating these discreet messages are available to industry
and commerce.

The area of training is probably the easiest application to
envisage. Descriptive scenes of routines and practices with
questions and answers supplied by the computer's text. Programmes can be paced by the student to suit his individual
needs. C.A.L. (Computer Assisted Learning) has perhaps not
been the success it was envisaged to be, because in its
software packages, the program was restricted to graphics and
text. The new dimension of pictures will add considerable
benefits to training needs. One has only to look at the work
currently being carried out by the Felix Viscom learning group
to see the potential of interactive learning systems. They
have already developed considerable skills in applying the
computer to video.

Merchandising too has been exploited by another London-based

company called Realmheath. They used video disc with the
Mothercare Group to help customers select product lines
available in the store. Mothercare are reported to be expanding their pilot project into all their 180 shops.

Corporate communications from some of our larger public
enterprises are likely to go the disc way in the not-too-
distant future. I have often told companies that I talk to
about this technology that interactive video communications
are contagious. A system may be considered for one area of
application at the intial contact stage but within a space
of a few months, other company needs are usually identified.
Once the system thinking process starts within organisations,
a multitude of uses can be identified. It should not be
thought that everyone in this seminar needs a computer-con-
trolled video disc system to enable them to perform their
business task more efficiently. That is certainly not the
case. I am not here today to sell the technology to anyone -
what I am saying, however, is: Be aware of this technology
and in time, work out whether there are significant applications that would warrant your organisations spending a lot
of money to prepare information for use with this medium.

Philips will start production on 'interactive' video disc
systems in the second half of next year.

These systems will include:

A video disc player;
computer interface (RS232 or IEEE);
Alpha numerical keyboard;
Teletext encoder;
Computer dump interpreter;
facilities for additional electronics e.g. sound-over still frame.

Today we are using pre-production systems on a prototype basis
in order that some key industries can obtain experience in using
interactive video discs coupled to computers.

6.   BUT WHAT WILL THE SYSTEM DO?

By using a Teletext encoder in our LaserVision system, we are
able to generate video text or computer graphics direct from the
player and display the video text over the picture coming from
the video discs.

This means that additional information in the form of video text
can be displayed to supplement picture information derived from
the video disc.

Obviously some data information is better communicated in a
textural form while other data may be more suited to still
pictures or moving pictures. LaserVision systems enable the
communications to be displayed in both forms, either separately

or by putting relevant text over picture. The text, unlike
the video disc information, can be updated at any time by
just changing the data base.

The computer program, of course, is also used to control
what visual information is displayed. By interfacing the
computer to the video disc player, an instruction can be
generated from the computer telling the disc to stop frame,
find a particular frame or sequence, play a sequence in slow
motion, speed up the display or alternate between the two
separate sound tracks that are available on the video disc.

In short, the total flexibility of this new communications
medium is significant. However, LaserVision systems should
not be considered as a communications medium unless a major
part of the information being communicated is in picture form.

7.   MAJOR ADVANTAGES OVER OTHER MEDIA

Other media that could be used for displaying high quality
pictures are: Film 16/35 mm; video tape.

Each of these standard formats have their own drawbacks.
Film deteriorates through use, a still frame can cause the
film to burn and rapid, random access is not possible. Video
tapes also deteriorates through use, and a still frame will
cause the head to wear out, and again, rapid random access
is not possible.

Video disc is unique in overcoming these problems of rapid
access, durability and still frame display.

8.   THE REAL COSTS OF USING A VIDEO MEDIUM

I have mentioned the kind of prices that discs cost and the
money involved here is rather small. But the costs incurred
in producing audio/visual software can be very high. Some
£30-40,000 can be involved in producing a relatively low-
cost production. Even where material already exists, for
example, 35 mm slides, the cost of transferring them to
professional video tape can be expensive.

To put visual information on to a video disc, it is first
necessary to transfer the original material e.g. film or
slide to a professional 1" broadcast quality video tape.
That is the medium we work from in our disc-making factory
in Blackburn. I have heard many commentators talk about
our disc being able to store over 50,000 individual frames,
a sort of Encyclopedia Britannica, but to transfer 50,000
pages to disc would probably cost in the region of half a
million pounds or £10 per slide.

There might well be applications where these software costs
are not so significant, for example in Defence work, or

Rogues' Gallery at Scotland Yard, but for the majority of
commercial applications, these prices are prohibitive.

9 . INTEGRATION WITH OTHER INFORMATION TECHNOLOGY

Today Viewdata is an industrial communications system quite
widely used by sections of industry. This means that data
bases have already been established and are regularly updated.

Companies already using Viewdata are usually the first org-
anizations to look at the communications benefits of Laser-
Vision. These companies often have a strong requirement for
high quality pictures coupled to their viewdata data base.
Obvious examples are the travel and tourist operators, car
manufacturers with large dealer networks and people in the
mail order business. Interestingly enough, representatives
from these three businesses are all talking here today on
Information Technology.

A possible handicap that should be mentioned in using Viewdata
with video information is that the two signals cannot be displayed together on the same screen. In some cases, of course,
this may not be required. Where the display of video text and
picture is simultaneously required, it would be necessary today
to down-load the viewdata information into a micro-computer and
then use the micro's floppy disc to interface with the Laser-
Vision system. The micro could of course be updated remotely
at regular intervals as it can interface with a viewdata data
base directly.

Companies like Owl Computers work closely with micro-computer
manufacturers, Apple in this case, to produce the necessary
boards to allow this interface between micros and viewdata.
Main frames and minis can, of course, be linked to the video
disc system in much the same way as a micro can, enabling
access to a much larger data base.

10. MILTON KEYNES DEVELOPMENT CORPORATION

Milton Keynes Development Corporation has just opened the
Information Technology House of the Future. This house will
be open for six months and we have installed one of our prototype LaserVision Systems there. The system is used to simulate
what the IT Screen of 1987 will be capable of showing and how
the household can use its screen in an interactive way. The
programme design was the responsibility of Butler Cox and
Partners with the production coming from the Open University
Production Centre. LaserVision is unique in being able to
offer this facility of fast random access to information on
the video disc, plus the generation of relevant video text and
computer control. The display in Milton Keynes is certainly
worth seeing.

11. FEASIBILITY STUDY

I think we all know that it is all too easy to get carried
away with the enthusiasm of new hi-tech. Some of you may
have done that in the early years with Prestel. But, as
with Prestel and any new communication medium, there is something to be said for having done it, or getting your feet wet.

While I make a point in my business discussions of talking
the majority of people out of thinking of using this technology - it's just not right for their application - I do en-
courage people with firm and practical ideas to carry out
feasibility studies involving pilot discs being made. We
in Philips will now offer project control and coordination and
act as a main contractor in producing the software packages
for customers.

The whole business of concept thinking, programme creation and
post production can be complex and our experience to date
suggests strongly to us that we have to be as involved with
the software as much as the hardware. We are in the systems
business.

12. CONCLUSION

In this Year of Information Technology, I am pleased that this
new business communications system has come to the final stage
of its development. Many companies other than Philips will be
supplying this technology to the market. Active partners are
Sony, Pioneer and Hitachi, although many other electronic
companies are developing this opto-electronic technology.

It is probably right to say that interactive video disc systems
will become as big over the next few years as micro computers
were in the late 1970's. After that, it's anybody's guess where
it will all take us.

INFORMATION ON SCREEN

David Wilson

I fear that it is rather bad form to begin talking about oneself.
But I hold rather strong views that it is essential for a communicator to identify himself right at the start, so that the receiver
can adjust himself or herself to the level and nature of what is
coming. So let me start by saying that I have held my present
position for exactly seven days, having previously worked as the
BBC's Science Correspondent. So you will understand that I have
only theory to offer and no experience - any attempt on my part
to claim knowledge you may safely discount as a mere journalistic
pose!

Nevertheless, I was directly involved exactly ten years ago
in the birth of Teletext. I got our News Information Library to
dig out the script. The date was October 25, 1972, almost precisely ten years ago. At that time, the BBC was celebrating its 50th
Anniversary, and it was in that context that we announced a new
development in broadcasting, and I went down to our Research Lab-
oratories at Kingswood Warren and filmed a news story on the invention of Ceefax. The research team in those days envisaged
putting out some thirty pages of text - nowadays, both BBC Ceefax
and ITV Oracle put out hundreds of pages.

But looking back on that ten year old script, it is quite
clear that I did not appreciate the enormous potential of what I
was seeing - and my only defence is that it seems that no one else
appreciated that potential either. Now, at the risk of boring many
of you, I want to repeat some of those things I learned that day
ten years ago.

Of course, I knew that television pictures were made up of
lines, 625 or 405 or whatever. What I did not know was that the
pictures we see as viewers do not use all the lines available. In
other words, the television signal we receive in our homes contains
blank spaces.

The original idea of Teletext was simply to use some of these
empty spaces to carry more information, and what the engineers and
scientists had done was to invent a way of putting signals on these
unused lines. These signals were a code which could be decoded by
a new device in your receiver and which would cause the television
set to produce on its screen a set of letters and numbers. Because
the code was put on unused lines, the letters could be sent at the
same time as the standard television programmes. In other words,
we can broadcast John Radcliffe's computer programmes at the same
time as we are broadcasting Jasper Carrott or Top of the Pops, and
you can receive them both at the same time.

I hope that I am not labouring the point, but I must point out

that Teletext is not the same as writing a set of words on some
caption or scroll and transmitting them by pointing a television
camera at the written material. In Teletext, the written word,
the writing, does not exist, theoretically, until it appears on
your screen. This apparently academic point is important in
considering the possibilities of Teletext.

It is precisely because this difference exists that Teletext has grown so rapidly and so separately. The originally
conceived thirty pages of news, weather and travel information
still exist, as you can see, on pages 101, 104, 137 and 182.
But there are all sorts of other things like the Top Ten (which
incidentally we also send to Austria). We can (and do) even
give creative writing its first airing, if you will pardon the
pun, on page 253. There is, of course, telesoftware on 704, 5 & 6.

The important point I want to make is this: that the original
discovery of ten years ago was in fact the discovery of a new
medium. My most distinguished predecessor, Colin McIntyre, the
man who more than any other 'created' Ceefax in the editorial
sense, coined the phrase 'printed radio'. I am tempted to go
further. I believe that Teletext is a new medium, the 'Broadcasting of the printed word'.

I do not want you to think that this is mere playing with
words. It has been a genuine point of trouble and confusion:
What have we got here? Teletext is broadcasting, no doubt
about that. It is not Viewdata - it is complementary to that.
But for those of us who are broadcasters, is it television, or
is it radio printed? It is both, in that radio broadcasts the
word and television broadcasts the picture. Teletext is, in fact,
itself, a new medium, the broadcasting of the printed word. And
it is the recognition of that which has brought my masters in the
BBC to set up my new unit, the Teletext unit. Something that can
broadcast things that were unthinkable ten years ago, like John
Radcliffe's computer programmes, which he described this morning,
our Telesoftware development. And of course subtitles for the
deaf and hard of hearing. By the way, if you think of subtitling
in terms of the things that used to appear on the screen during
French or Polish films, think again and have a look at a BBC
programme with subtitles, like the present series of Tenko, and
you will see such a leap of sophistication that it's a pity we
haven't thought up a new name to describe something which is
qualitatively different.

I would like to pursue this theme of a new medium a little
further. Librarians are the keepers of humanity's database. I
know many of this audience are in charge of technical library
facilities, those sections of information which we more commonly
think of as databases. But in literature of the kind we call
'artistic', we also have a database on human experience, a database of the experiences, emotions and reactions of other human
beings to varying situations of human life. This recording is
the role of writing in literate societies. Now in Teletext, we

have a new and enormously powerful mode of access to this database. Let me put it in this slightly fantastical way - Teletext could perfectly well broadcast ten pages a day of some great classical work of literature. We could make Pride and Prejudice Book of the Week, or Gibbon's 'Decline and Fall' Book of the Year. What I am thinking towards is not that we will literally do these things, but if you think of what we were told this morning about the Optical Videodisc, and you think about Teletext, the traditional view of the book, this is the binding together of paper pages to be read by the individual sitting in a quiet room at home, is becoming blurred at the edges. The book and broadcasting are beginning to merge together.

Enough of these flights of fancy - I have indulged in them simply to provoke you into considering that Teletext is a good deal more important than just a fast way of getting <u>real</u> information, which only librarians have at hand, on to distant desks. Teletext is now and will remain a method of broadcasting information, and it will always have as one of its main contents the provision of news. You will forgive me as an ex-journalist for believing that news is information. But as I hope I showed you earlier, there is much more information available on Teletext now than just the news, even when you use that word in its broadest context. Information in the computer-man's sense of the word will be coming shortly with Telesoftware as John Radcliffe has explained.

I suggest you should think of Teletext in terms of what Gutenberg and Caxton achieved - we are at the very beginning of a new medium.

We are aware that Teletext has rather Gutenberg-style deficiencies and our engineering and research scientists have ideas about rectifying them. What about the content? And what about such problems as what the viewer actually wants? These are things which we have to think about editorially, or professionally, and I would be very interested to hear what anybody here thinks about the contents of Teletext.

Teletext, like any other invention of information technology, obeys the basic computer rule: Garbage In; Garbage Out. Believe me, it cannot be run on a shoe string. It has to have first rate journalists etc to provide its imput, and it has to have access itself to first-rate sources of information. I would add that audience research for Teletext usage is not easy, as you can imagine if you think how you would set about it yourselves.

There are other questions which engage our attention. What is the best way of showing the receiver, the viewer, what he can find and where and how to find it? This is certainly something we have not yet solved, in my view.

Another problem we have to think about is one which will be familiar to many of this audience, our library. I suppose if I were to talk about shelf-space and finance, it would bring a wry grin to most faces here and you would mutter: 'what is this chap talking about this for, I know far more about it than he does'. You would of course be right, so I won't talk about it, beyond pointing out that your problem is a problem for us too. I think I'm right in saying that our computer has a library of six thousand pages, so what shelf-space is that, for a machine that is turning out six hundred pages all the time, pages which are being changed regularly as the News changes, or as the weather prospects change, and which are changed almost everyday in any case. I say no more at the moment than that this is a problem we have to think about.

But there is one more thing that I must mention about Teletext as Information on the Screen. And that is speed, or more accurately, speed of change. Information on the Screen means most of the time, and especially to technical people, the provision of information on a screen from a fairly fixed database. The difference for Teletext, the broadcasting of the printed word, is that only some of its information comes into that standard category. Much of Teletext's information is of a rapidly changing variety, news in the ordinary sense, of course, but equally important details about traffic blockages and which trains are running if there is a transport strike, not irrelevant information today, you may agree.

Now, it is an unspoken understanding in academic life that fast-moving information is of little value. It is dismissed as ephemeral. I speak with some personal feeling here, for I am the journalistic black sheep of a largely respectable academic family. This is not the place to enter my arguments against this valuation of immediate information. Let me simply say that if any of you try that one on, you will find I have a battery of fierce arguments against it. Nevertheless, this unspoken set of standards remains - a hardback book is somehow better, more reliable, than a paperback; but a paperback lauds it over an article in a monthly journal, and that in turn must be more 'considered' than an article in a weekly. A Third programme talk comes somewhere about this level, and lower down, we come to the newspaper article. Down at the bottom comes a piece on television, the most ephemeral of all media. I am simply asking you to reconsider the matter. And I will go on to suggest that Teletext will necessarily disrupt this standard of judgement.

Graham Clayton, who is now Editor of Ceefax, and who kindly stood down to let me introduce myself to you, had chosen as his title 'A Dream Come True'. That is very apt. I've tried to let you see some of my dreams about Teletext. So let me end with W B Yeats: 'Tread softly for you tread on my dreams'.

WEST MIDLANDS VIEWDATA EXPERIMENT

Pat Montague

Seven years ago I spoke to Aslib on a topic called 'Computers in Newspapers and their Implications for Newspaper Libraries'. Today I am talking to you again because of my Company's involvement in computers and electronic publishing. Computers and their extensive use in our newspapers are a key part in our means of survival - electronic publishing and in particular, viewdata, is our door to the future.

The Birmingham Post and Mail has been involved in viewdata since the start of the original pilot trial by British Telecom late in 1975. The West Midlands Residential project, or Club 403, is, to us, the most exciting and practical attempt to develop a package for the residential user during those seven years. However, before I give you a detailed resume of that project, let me give you a brief outline of my company, its publishing activities and the background to its present position in electronic publishing.

Our operation in Birmingham is the largest independent newspaper publishing centre outside the national newspapers in England. Our newspapers comprise:

The Birmingham Evening Mail - nearly 300,000 copies daily, with 21 editions and 6 advertising zones; its household penetration is of the order of 50% and it has the highest readership of any evening newspaper outside London in the UK;

The Birmingham Post - a serious, up-market morning newspaper selling some 36,000 copies daily, with heavy emphasis on business and finance;

The Sunday Mercury - a unique Sunday newspaper distributed over the whole of the West Midlands region, with a sale of some 170,000 copies;

The Saturday Sports Argus - is the largest circulation Saturday evening sports paper in the UK with a sale of nearly 60,000 copies.

These four newspapers have been the bedrock of our traditional role as printed word publishers. More recently, we have added ten free weekly newspapers, totalling some 300,000 copies weekly, and providing purely locality advertising, news and information. We have been constantly aware of the need for involvement in new alternative media from as early as the 1950's, when we took the maximum allowable investment in ATV through ACC. In the 1970's, we headed up a consortium which won the local commercial radio franchise and now have this as a further investment in the future.

At the same time as these changes have been going on, we have been investing heavily in bringing ourselves forward from the 19th century into the 1980's, with some £3m being spent on capital and software over the last eight years in text handling systems alone, and a total of some £8m in enhancing our printing and publishing capabilities.

The investment decisions in 1974 and subsequently have been based upon a control database philosophy. This in turn has been based upon the belief that electronic and other printed media would require the re-use of already keyboarded material. This approach was reconfirmed late in 1975 with the announcement of the British Telecom Viewdata pilot study. We became information providers then, although in all honesty, we did very little other than act as observers until late 1977. Our involvement at that stage was based upon fear, fear of the promise of a cheap alternative mass media, damaging or removing key revenue categories in, for example, classified advertising and abbreviated news and information services delivered direct to the home.

That fear has now eased. However, fear is a great motivator and in consequence, since 1978, we have invested considerable time effort and finance in developing an information and interactive package on Prestel suitable to meet the needs and aspirations of people both at work and at home, through our electronic publishing service, Viewtel 202. The success of our operation is demonstrated by the fact that since January 1981, we have had over 10% of all accesses to IP databases on Prestel, with scarcely 2% of the pages. Our objective has been the mass market, and our efforts have been geared to being able to meet that market's needs when the time became ripe. The user is our living. Club 403 will be a significant step in that direction, representing the first truly coordinated approach by all sides of the viewdata industry to developing a residential viewdata package. It will seek to answer most, if not all, Scott Maynes' criticisms of Prestel on routing and ease of access to information.

Club 403's origins arise from the DOI's initiatives through our Chairman today, Ric Foot, to stimulate a more rapid development in Teletext. This stimulus has been so successful that, from a stumbling, painfully slow development for over five years, the last twelve months have seen teletext become the standard for 22" sets and above for rental in the UK, with over 800,000 likely to be installed by the New Year.

In February 1982, the DOI called together all sides of the Viewdata industry, from TV manufacturers, renters and retailers to information providers from private viewdata suppliers to Prestel, from electronic chip manufacturers to consultants. Out of that meeting has come Club 403.

What is Club 403? It is a package of information and services specifically aimed at the residential consumer, using the latest in modern electronic technology, via the Prestel network.

The opportunities it offers are: 1. to examine what the residential consumer requires from such a service and to

establish what they are prepared to pay for it;
2.   To examine the practical issues involved in a test market
     situation from the point of view of the information and
     service provider;
3.   To examine the future implications on current trading methods
     and to maximise the opportunities presented by Information
     Technology.

The benefits of this particular project are:
1.   Government support in pump priming and co-ordinating;
2.   Prestel support;
3.   TV manufacturer and trade support;
4.   Generic marketing campaign;
5.   Comprehensive research programme;
6.   Database design and control based upon proven experience.

This boils down to a united team approach to meet the users' and
service providers' needs.

CLUB 403 Timetable

October - December 1982:	Agreement with service providers to participate
	Decision as to services to be made available
	Finalisation of technical/operational issues
	Formulation of 'page' presentation on screen
January - February 1983:	Pilot research programme with 100+ users
March - August:	Test market operation
	Evaluation

     Before I move on to the Club 403 proposition, I will assume
that the audience understands the mechanics of Prestel, its merits
and its deficiencies.

Public Viewdata - The Service

     The component parts of public viewdata are as follows:

     British Telecom, providing the network;
     Prestel providing the viewdata system and computer;
     TV equipment manufacturers and distributors, providing the
               hardware;
     Prestel IP's, providing services and information on the
               service.

At present:

     Prestel operates for 24 hours a day, 7 days a week;

There are currently 20,000 Prestel sets in all (85% of which
    are business users);
1/4 million pages are instantly accessible on the medium;
over 1000 information providers are responsible for these
    pages;
more than 60% of the population are within local call reach
of the Prestel network.

As a publishing and advertising medium, features include:
full service and information provider control of on-screen presentation; efficient information retrieval via direct page access,
directories, menu-type indexes and, in the future, more advanced
search techniques; precise viewing and marketing information.

As an interactive communicator, features include:
Teleshopping - orders   - opinion sampling
              - bookings   - home banking
              - data collection

Mailbox   - user to user message service

The reasons why we should be looking at a mass market now are:
falling hardware costs; falling residential connection costs; service provider-led initiatives accelerating residential market
opportunities; full, real-time transactional processing through to
third party computers now being available; and the opportunity for
service providers to develop new markets for products and services
relatively cheaply.

What then is the Club 403 proposition? Many interested parties
are looking to develop the potential involved in facilitation electronic transactions of all kinds, using the familiar television set.
The questions being raised today are not so much whether this will
happen or not, but rather when, how and what are the implications
for the future of retail and other types of domestic and business
transaction, plus social reformation for the community.

The Department of Industry has recognised the significance of
such developments on the country's economy, and has agreed to assist
industry and commerce in their efforts to accelerate this process,
and to endeavour to find the answers to some of these very funde-
mental questions.

Bearing in mind the magnitude of the objective, and the im-
portance of success, it is proposed that a pilot research operation should be mounted, whereby first hand experience can be secured
with the domestic consumer in his own home.

The principal objectives of the 'test market' are as follows:
1.   To find out whether there is a significant market for residen-
     tial viewdata services;
2.   To find out what the consumer requires from such a service;
3.   To find out what the consumer is prepared to pay for such a
     service;
4.   To stimulate industry, trade, social information providers and

consumer interest in the realities of such a proposition.

'CLUB 403', as the test market will be known, will use Prestel viewdata technology, allowing commercial enterprise and social information providers the undoubted benefits of being able to talk to their customers in the relaxed atmosphere of their own home, via the system.

The concept of CLUB 403 will be to offer customers a tailor-made package of news, information and services, designed to help them in their everyday lives. The package will comprise the following: the world's first electronic newspaper, covering inter-national/national sport and local news; information on local and social services; opportunities for transactions via the TV set; message facilities; entertainment.

In order to test this concept out at a manageable and yet realistic and worthwhile level, it is intended to concentrate efforts as follows:
- in the West Midlands area (Edgbaston/Solihull/Sutton Coldfield);
- in 2500 homes (A/B/C1 socio-demographic groupings), the normal group for the evolution of new high technology;
- public access terminals will also be looked at;
- using local editorial and database management through ourselves;
- charging a flat rate consumer subscription for the service (plus the cost of local telephone calls, which is likely to be £4.00 per month);
- offering discounted hardware for a six months' promotional period at teletext prices.

In support of the above, a comprehensive, co-ordinated, mar-keting campaign will be mounted, and an extensive research programme will be undertaken to monitor and evaluate the full implications of the programme.

The mechanics of CLUB 403 will be as follows: initial consumer research indicates that there are a number of elements of a basic residential viewdata package which would inspire customers to purchase the facility. These are as follows:

* Teleshopping   * Leisure
* Housekeeping   * Club Membership
* Education   * DIY

The package will be developed and marketed in such a way as to cover all these elements and will determine any order of preference on the part of consumers in terms of providing an effective 'trigger' to purchase.

Meanwhile, the database itself is being developed to encompass two main facilities: those which are purely information-orientated; and those which lead to transactional applications, requiring customer response. For example, extensive information services including: regional, national and international news and weather; travel information, including train and plane timetables, plus holiday availability; home maintenance/DIY; commodity shopping list; educational information and services; leisure, including games, sports and hobbies; social services; classified advertising, with conversion of existing printed classifieds to viewdata format on a key word structure basis; or services offering opportunities for customer response, including: commodity shopping; mail order shopping; banking; emergency services; user to user messages; hotel and theatre bookings etc; holiday and travel bookings etc.

Discussions are currently taking place with virtually every major retailer, mail order house and financial institution you can imagine. A group called SIPG or Social Information Providers Group is examining what social information should be put up. To give you just a taste of those committed to participate, these include: GUS, Curry's, Debenhams, Met Office, American Express, two major clearing banks, two building societies, one insurance company and the National Bus Company. Supermarket discussions are also well advanced.

Monitoring the test market operation from the point of view of both the TV trade and the providers of services and information is a fundamentally important and valuable part of the programme, in order to ascertain how these services might best be marketed nationally.

As a basic premise for the research programme, answers to the following key questions will be sought:

- Who is the best demographic target group for a package such as CLUB 403?
- How often do consumers use CLUB 403 and for what purpose?
- Does use of the service change/develop with greater familiarity?
- What problems are there with such a package and how can these be resolved?
- What are the principal benefits for trade and industry?
- What are the effects upon existing printed media services of information?

Methodology: The Pilot Study

Experience with Teletext and Prestel is valuable in providing information about the key attributes to be included in the test market. Notwithstanding broad agreement on the content of the package, the precise positioning of the new service requires careful consideration, in order to ensure maximum initial and continuing impact with the public.

For this reason, an initial pilot group of approximately 100 households will be recruited in order to explore these issues,

which are   particularly vital in the light of the totally new
concept to be communicated. The pilot groups will be started in
January 1983, with initial attitudes and expectations of the service being explored before the actual set is installed in the
household.

These pilot groups will be reconvened during the course of
the test market period, to evaluate how their attitudes and usage
have changed with increased familiarity of the service.

The information gathered from these pilot groups will be
used in the development of questionnaires for the main test market monitor, as well as in the development of the services offered
on CLUB 403.

The Test Market

It is anticipated that some 2500 consumer households will
participate in the test market.

Some aspects of the research/monitor are to be undertaken by
the Project Team, in conjunction with the TV trade. The majority,
however, will be handled by a specialised experienced research
agency.

Research Package for Information and Service Providers

It is the intention to supply information and service providers
with a regular flow of research data, plus analysis of consumer usage
and attitudes to the package, both in general as well as with specific
relevance to a provider's own service.

Key features will include: weekly reports and analysis on viewdata set universe, page access and usage; four monthly reports on
consolidated weekly data, plus diary analysis, telephone summary
analysis, qualitative management summary (and specific supplier data
at cost where required); two quarterly reports on consolidated
monthly data, plus project review (and again, specific supplier data
at cost if required).

Marketing Support

The CLUB 403 Project Team, together with the Department of
Industry, will be co-ordinating marketing activity in support of
the operation. It is believed that this is an extremely important
aspect, the principal objective being to stimulate consumer interest
and ensure that this is carried through to a strong high street
presence.

Specifically, the Project Team are designing a corporate
identity for the package, together with a generic marketing and
publicity campaign.

It is anticipated that individual companies participating in the operation will see fit to supplement this basic programme and use the generic theme to mount their own complementary marketing activity.

The following is a summary of the basic marketing activity that is envisaged as forming part of the generic programme.

1.   In-Store Material for TV Trade Outlets

To ensure brief of showroom staff and service engineers, each outlet in the area will receive a number of trade folders containing the necessary material to ensure a full briefing.

To attract and educate/sell to consumers, a selection of point of sale material and merchandising material will be produced.

To motivate showroom staff, a series of trade display competitions and sales incentive schemes will be mounted in which showrooms will be encouraged to participate.

2.   In-Store Material for Local Services Providers

Again, a package of literature and merchandising material will be made available to all these outlets.

Furthermore, to motivate these outlets, a series of trade display competitions and tailormade promotions will be mounted. A small display/demonstration stand will be made available if required.

3.   Local Advertising/Public Relations

The campaign will include the following:
* Local radio advertising) both with the possibility of
* Local press advertising) links with trade activity
* Editorial coverage on local TV and local press TV page
* Door to door leaflets   * Posters
* Public place demonstration (eg shopping precinct)
* Schools and other local community activity
* Branded stationery for use by Project Team and individual
   outlets as required.

4.   Consumer Launch Pack

The 2500 consumer sample will be given a package of information and merchandising material on entering the project.

In summary, then, I would suggest to you that 1983 will see the first stage of the development of a residential public service viewdata market on Prestel, with major opportunities for all sections of commerce and social information. 1984 onwards will then offer the real opportunity to expand and build on the foundations created over the next twelve months.

B L'S PRIVATE VIDEOTEX SERVICE

Geoff Hutt

BLSL initially set up a private Videotex service to give thirty
users access to a single application, Stock Locator, which showed
the position of virtually all unsold BL cars throughout the UK.
The demand for other applications generated by this information
retrieval facility caused BLSL to expand their service rapidly
to carry a wide range of systems, accessed by several hundred
users.

The original impetus for the installation of a Videotex
service came from the realisation by the Sales and Marketing
Department of BL Cars that there was a real danger of a communications gap developing between the company and its dealer network. Within the UK, BL sells cars through a network of about
1700 dealers. The relationship between BL and its dealers is
that of independent commercial organisations but is complicated
by a number of factors viz:

1.   The geographic dispersion of the network throughout the
      country;
2.   The disparity in size and sophistication between the largest
      and the smallest outlets; and
3.   The ownership of some garage groups by multinational companies
      as large or larger than BL itself.

Despite these complications, BL sells over 250,000 cars per
year through this diverse network. Furthermore, each car is the
subject of numerous interchanges of information, from the original
forecast of sale, through to warranty registration. Many systems
applications thus involved both BL and the dealers, linking them
by different communications media. Since there had not been an
overall communications strategy in existence, as each new application had been developed, a new link in the chain had been forged.
Rationalisation had, of course, been carried out, but this is no
substitute for a strategy. BL Cars was therefore concerned that
the right person was not always being supplied with the right
information at the right time.

They therefore turned to BLSL for help, first to provide an
analysis of the problem and then recommendations as to its solution.

BLSL examined three alternatives:

1.   Enhancing existing links;
2.   Enlarging their conventional teleprocessing network;
3.   Establishing a Videotex service.

The first alternative was rapidly discarded, as current post/
telephone/telex links were people-dependent, and hence would become

less dependable and more expensive in the future. As sophisticated users of interactive computing, with vast experience in
manufacturing, engineering and commercial areas, BLSL considered
the second alternative very favourably. This was made more attrac-
tive since much of the information either emanated from or returned
to the central computer files. This idea, however, ran into problems with the end users; the small dealers did not want to become
involved with computing and the large dealers had already installed
non-compatible equipment. BLSL therefore considered the use of
Videotex to overcome these objections, offering cheap general
purpose terminals that were easy to install and use.

The concept was shown to Sales and Marketing management, who
sponsored the creation of a demonstration package for the Sales
Panel, a cross section of the dealer community. The Panel recomm-
ended that BL proceed with Videotex and thus the service was
launched on a pilot basis, offering a single application, Stock
Locator, to a cross section of dealers.

The response was so enthusiastic that the service was
expanded to cover several hundred dealers. The emplacement of
this dedicated, information retrieval application created demand
in several quarters, i e:

1. BL Sales and Marketing grasped the opportunity to transfer
    other existing applications to Videotex, where there were
    identifiable benefits.

2. They also launched other applications which had not prev-
    iously been possible under existing communications links,
    e g to provide links between despatch and control areas
    during the launch of new vehicles.

3. The dealers themselves asked for a growing number of
    applications, using increasingly sophisticated facilities,
    which brought about the introduction of Closed User Groups
    on to the service.

4. Other functional areas within BL took advantage of the comm-
    unications ability which had been created, and used it to
    meet previously unsatisfied demands, eg the collection of
    data for Pensions files and the dissemination of company in-
    formation.

BLSL has therefore capitalised on the original dedicated service, and used it to generate significant volumes of business that
it would otherwise not have expected to receive.

The service, however, still continues to evolve. A trial application is now allowing for the rapid exchange of information between
BL's sales organisation in this country and its subsidiaries on the
Continent. This is regarded as just the prelude to a large, international network, with the potential to penetrate every BL market.

Within BLSL, Videotex is now seen as a standard technique in its armoury, an important tool in the continuing migration of systems functions from being data processors to becoming information communicators.

TELESHOPPING

David Bird

David Bird's presentation included: a) a Video Film of
Telephone Ordering; b) several slides describing various
aspects of GUS business; c) a live demonstration of an
audio response telephone order in Kays; d) a live demonstration of a Viewdata order in BMOC. Since the demonstration element played such a vital part in his presentation, he felt a transcript would be either unintelligible
or a distortion of the paper he gave. For this reason,
no further details are given.

BRITAIN ON PRESTEL

David Barr

Introduction

The main focus of my paper is on information systems and services, rather than on technology as such. In the context of Prestel, this is an important distinction, because that is only one of many tools used in our overall information system which is in turn deployed to provide an information service to identified sets of users.

Several references have already been made during this conference to Prestel's failure to achieve the ambitious targets set for it; I would like to suggest that part of the reason for this failure is that Prestel has too often been presented as an information system, whereas in fact it is merely a set of components making up a communications vehicle, on to which can be built information systems and services. Those services still need to be created with all the care and skill which go into services provided through other media, and to an audience of librarians, I think it fair to say that it is the absence of the kind of information skills which you can provide which is the most important missing factor on Prestel. Too many amateur information services have been attempted.

The most glaring difficulty of all has been the absence of adequate indexing, leading to poorly structured databases and poor retrieval capabilities. The projects I shall describe to you a little later are in fact two large-scale indexing projects created to provide one good central index in the form of an alphabetical gazetteer of British towns, and to build on that an integrated BRITAIN database from the material of the British Tourist Authority, British Council and Central Office of Information, all of whom represent Britain officially overseas, and have additional specific domestic responsibilities.

BTA's Information System

To reinforce my opening statement, it is important that you know a little about BTA's overall information systems and services by way of explaining why we use viewdata at all.

The British Tourist Authority is Britain's national tourist office. Its main responsibility is for promoting tourism from overseas to Britain, although it does have the complementary responsibility for some activities in this country, which it implements in association with the domestic tourist boards of England, Scotland, Wales and Northern Ireland. It has a budget of about £25 million, £18 million coming from Government as grant-in-aid, and the balance from our own commercial activities. We are one of those commercial organisations who, quite correctly, are required to work in close association with the very large private sector in our industry, and create many of our most effective projects as joint ventures. This is very relevant to the way in which we have developed our Prestel activities.

There are approximately twelve million overseas visitors coming to Britain each year, generating earnings of £4000 million in foreign currency, a huge contribution to the 'invisible' sector of the balance of trade. BTA's information services deals directly with over 1.5 million enquiries, and the travel trade handle many more using information supplied by us.

The reasons for having an information service may seem obvious, but they are in fact as follows:

1. The public and travel trade do ask questions in very large numbers and expect answers to be provided.

2. Information is an essential 'lubricant' to selling travel and tourism; it is a promotional weapon in its own right.

3. Information also constitutes an after-sales service, when frequently more detailed information is again required. A good after-sales service generates repeat business, which is certainly a characteristic of our tourist traffic. Britain's excellent tourist 'product' is the main factor; information about it is also a contributory factor.

4. Information is needed as an input to printed publications. Despite advances in electronic publishing, print will remain the main promotional medium for a long time yet.

Print is, however, not so effective for servicing enquiries for specific information, and there is a very great demand for specific information. Traffic to this country is 20% business, 80% leisure; of that 80%, nearly 85% is defined as 'independent', i.e. people have not bought fully inclusive packages. The implication is that they buy many of the components of a total holiday in separate pieces, and also that they may well buy part of their holiday after their arrival in Britain. The information system needs therefore to have fairly specific retrieval capabilities.

Information Flow, Processing and Dissemination

The sources of the data for the information system are very diverse, which often means that it comes in very diverse formats, and requires considerable processing before it can be deployed for use by BTA. The sources are tourist boards, local authorities, tour operators, carriers, special interest associations, hotel groups, small businesses and individuals, press publications, brochures and many other miscellaneous items. All of this has to be acquired and processed in the shortest possible time to retain its real value on the timescales involved in international promotions. Storage and processing ranges from the conventional paper files, card indexes, manuals, information library to word processing, computerised database management and typesetting, and viewdata.

Before reaching any of the technical processing systems, the data has to come to one of the three product information units dealing with accommodation, travel and events. Rather like academic literature, each specialism within these broad labels has its own characteristics which must be overcome by the relevant information officer.

The overwhelming challenge for all of them is the timescale issue. Events information may be required for long-haul territories like Japan or Australia some eighteen months or more before the event itself. Print is a cumbersome, expensive, and time-consuming method of transmitting information and keeping it up to date, and it is in this aspect of our work that electronic media will play an increasing role in the future.

In addition to that, a general theme which has emerged throughout this conference - and one which is certainly true of the travel industry - is that in five years' time, it will be a very sterile exercise indeed to provide an information service on travel which does not include details of up-to-date availability and a transactions function for booking/reserving and paying for the product. Already our operations are moving in that direction with the establishment with commercial partners of British Travel Centres in Frankfurt, Amsterdam, Oslo and Brussels. By using electronic media, we are in fact increasingly able to provide a supermarket of travel and tourism to Britain within very modest premises.

Why use Prestel?

Prestel is one of several media which offer potentially cost-effective ways of providing widespread access to frequently changing information. The biggest disappointment of course with Prestel at the moment as a public viewdata system is that it really does not have the size of audience which would normally attract a higher standard of information provision.

Within specific contexts, Prestel can have a vital role in matching supply and demand by simply providing information. During the Jubilee celebrations, for example, the very damaging story got out that London was full. It never was, but there was no information on availability of hotel rooms, which could have been made available via Prestel. Even better would be the services made possible by Gateway, i.e. access to third party computers already dedicated to the business of transacting reservations. This is also very relevant to the servicing of independent travellers whom I mentioned earlier. Not only that, but a great deal of the servicing will be handled on a self-service basis in locations like banks, post offices and public libraries etc, using coin-operated sets.

That is why we use Prestel. We have at the moment 7000 frames on Prestel, and plans for further expansion through two major projects.

Britain Gazetteer and BRITAIN Database

The first project is to create a major gazetteer of Britain on
Prestel to serve as a central geographical index for both our
database and for other information on Prestel. To this index
can be linked detailed information about the facilities and services available in those towns. The second project, which grows
out of the first, is to work with our partners at the British
Council and the Central Office of Information to develop an integrated BRITAIN database. There is no obvious reason why the
typical user should know where the responsibilities of these
organisations begin and end, so it would be more effective to
produce a coordinated 'official' database on Britain.

        Let's look first at the gazetteer. The opening frame
looks like this:

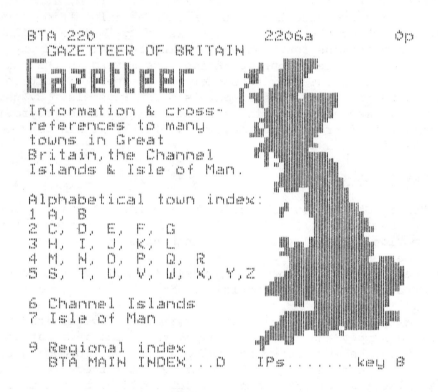

If we take the example of BRISTOL, we follow through two frames:

```
BTA 220                          220601a          0p
      BRITAIN GAZETTEER
      Alphabetical Index of Towns

  1 Abb - Alt

  2 Amb - Ash

  3 Ath - Az
    B - Barm

  4 Barm - Bee

  5 Bel - Bis

  6 Bla - Bow

  7 Bra - Brom

  8 Brom - Bux

                      GAZETTEER INDEX...9
```

```
BTA 220                          220601?a         0p
      BRITAIN GAZETTEER
      Alphabetical Index
  11 Brackley
  12 Bracknell        51 Bridlington
  13 Bradford         52 Bridport
  14 Bradford-on-     53 Brightlingsea
        Avon          54 Brighton
  15 Braemar          61 Brill
  21 Braintree        62 Bristol
  ▥  Bramhall         63 Brixham
  ▥  Brampton         71 Broadstairs
  ▥  Braunton         72 Broadway
  31 Brecon           73 Brockenhurst
  32 Brentwood        74 Brodick
  41 Bridgend         81 Bromley
  42 Bridgnorth       82 Bromsgrove
  43 Bridgwater       83 Bromyard

  Towns in white: one page of
                  information only
                  GAZETTEER INDEX...9
```

... to the Bristol town page

```
BTA 220                          220614a        Op
     Bristol
     Avon                   Population 411,800

     0 Tourist notes
     1 Travel and Transport
     2 Accommodation and Restaurants
     3 Activities/Entertainments/Events
     4 Local Businesses
     6 Education and Training
     7 Local and Community Information
     Information will be added as available
     under: Other Information
▐▐▐▐▐▐▐▐▐▐▐▐▐▐▐▐▐▐▐▐▐▐▐▐▐▐▐▐▐▐▐▐▐▐▐▐▐▐▐▐▐▐▐▐

Market Fri,Sat   Early closing Wed,Sat
City just off the M4, 88 miles south
west of Birmingham, 113 miles west of
London. Cardiff 44 miles, Exeter 75.
Railway station provides 125 High Speed
Train services to London.
                    GAZETTEER INDEX....9
```

There are gaps, at no. 5, for example, to leave us some flexibility
until the appropriate headings can be established. If we now take
the travel and transport sector, we go through the range of choices
available:

```
BTA 220                          2206141a       Op
     BRISTOL
     Travel and Transport

RAIL TRAVEL
1 BRITISH RAIL— timetable,services and
     fares to/from London
COACH TRAVEL
2 NATIONAL EXPRESS - Details of
     principal services and fares from
     Bristol

AIR TRAVEL
5 ABC - Scheduled air services
6 DAN-AIR - flights from Bristol
CAR HIRE
7 AMERICAN EXPRESS -info on car hire
     rates,petrol,tyres and parts
8 KENNING CAR HIRE - Self drive and
     Chauffeur drive


,,,,,,,,,,,,,, Bristol front page..0
```

and key 1 which takes us out of the gazetteer and into the British
Rail database.

```
British Rail              221703350a    Op
LDN PADDINGTON⇔BRISTOL -PARKWAY/TEMPLE
MDS-WESTON S.M Mon-Fri 4/10-13/5/83
dep     arr     arr     arr
PADD    B.PW    B.TM    W.SM    notes

0700    0826    -- --   -- --   mb
0740    -- --   0916    1000a   b*
0810    0921    -- --   -- --   mr
0815    -- --   0941    1036a   mrb*
0840    -- --   1024    1046    b
0910    1015    -- --   -- --   r
0915    -- --   1040    1114a   b*
0945    1104    -- --   -- --   r
1015    -- --   1146    1247a   b
1040    -- --   1225    -- --   b

BR Index 0  Return 1   Sat 2   Sun 3
later trains 4
fares B.P Way 6 B.T Meads 7 Weston 8
NOTES (Standard notes Key 9)
CHANGES a Bristol Temple meads
```

If we go back to the town page

```
BTA 220                   220614a      Op
    Bristol
    Avon              Population 411,800

0 Tourist notes
1 Travel and Transport
2 Accommodation and Restaurants
3 Activities/Entertainments/Events
4 Local Businesses
5 Education and Training
7 Local and Community Information
Information will be added as available
under: Other Information
▒▒▒▒▒▒▒▒▒▒▒▒▒▒▒▒▒▒▒▒▒▒▒▒▒▒▒▒▒▒▒▒▒▒▒▒▒▒▒▒▒▒▒▒▒▒▒

Market Fri,Sat   Early closing Wed,Sat
City just off the M4, 88 miles south
west of Birmingham, 113 miles west of
London. Cardiff 44 miles, Exeter 75.
Railway station provides 125 High Speed
Train services to London.
            GAZETTEER INDEX....9
```

and select route 2 to accommodation and restaurants

```
BTA 220                      2206142a      0p
   BRISTOL
   Accommodation and Restaurants


HOTELS
1 ROOMWATCH - Where to stay
2 HOLIDAY INN - Full details of rates,
   facilities and services

4 AMERICAN EXPRESS - Guide to hotels
5 ALPHA 460 - the Ship Post Hotel,
   Bristol,bookable via Prestel
6 ROOMSERVICE 678 - Choose and BOOK
   your hotel using Prestel

RESTAURANTS
7 AMERICAN EXPRESS - restaurants

9 ALPHA 460 - continental restaurants


             Bristol front page..0
```

and take route 6 into the Roomwatch service which deals exclusively
with hotels which can be booked, we get not only a choice of hotels
but also a routing line back to the gazetteer, a reciprocal cross
reference which we hope to make a standard feature of the gazetteer...

```
ROOMSERVICE 678        67822112a      0p
Bristol



1 Grand Hotel **** Broad Street
2 Holiday Inn **** Old Market
3 Grosvenor Hotel Victoria Street




8 British Tourist Authority Gazetteer
9 Avon        0 Roomservice Main Index
```

Selecting the Grand Hotel, Key 1, and leave Roomservice to enter
the database of AVS Intext who put up the information about the
Grand Hotel.

```
AVS INTEXT                    2768011a      Op
   GRAND HOTEL                Tel: 0272 291645
   BROAD ST., BRISTOL,                  **** STAR
   BS1 2EL, AVON                        180 rooms

LOCATION: Close to city centre. Train
station 1m, airport 7m, motorway 1m.

NEARBY PLACES OF INTEREST: Cotswold
villages 40m, Bath 11m, Clifton Suspen-
sion Bridge 2m.

FACILITIES: Rest, bar, free parking,
public bar serving real ales, whole
Hotel beautifully refurbished. Some
pets allowed.

TARIFF: from 1/10/82
Single   £35.65     Price includes VAT &
Double   £48.30     English breakfast.

   Key 1 Conference Facilities
       2 Getaway Breaks 0 Reservations
```

Key zero for the booking frame

```
AVS INTEXT                    276B0110a      Op
   This is a booking form for THE GRAND
   HOTEL. Please complete as indicated.
   Confirmation will be by phone within
   one working day.

NUMBER OF ROOMS REQUIRED:
Single            Double/Twin

ARRIVING DATE:(ddmmyy)
DURATION:          NIGHTS

GUEST'S NAME OR TELEPHONE EXTENSION NO.

If booking a Getaway Break, key 1
To order Hotel brochure, key 1
To order a Conference Pack, key 1
   BRITISH TOURIST AUTHORIT
   239 OLD MARYLEBONE-
   ROAD
   LONDON
   NW1 5QT
   01 724 0449        WED 26 JAN 1983 10:32
```

fill it in,

```
AVS INTEXT                27680110a      Op
   This is a booking form for THE GRAND
   HOTEL. Please complete as indicated.
   Confirmation will be by phone within
   one working day.

NUMBER OF ROOMS REQUIRED:
Single          Double/Twin   1

ARRIVING DATE:(ddmmyy)
DURATION:      1   NIGHTS

GUEST'S NAME OR TELEPHONE EXTENSION NO.

If booking a Getaway Break, Key 1
To order Hotel brochure, Key 1      1
To order a Conference Pack, Key 1   1
 BRITISH TOURIST AUTHORIT
 PRESTEL UNIT
 239 OLD MARYLEBONE
              ROAD

LONDON
 01 262 0141      WED 23 FEB 1983 12:26
KEY 1 TO SEND, KEY 2 NOT TO SEND
```

and the transaction is completed.

   I have illustrated this example through the alphabetical
gazetteer of Britain, but in addition, the same point is quickly
reached by using the main Prestel regional routes, as follows:

```
P R E S T E L             3a          Op
Britain

▓▓▓▓▓▓▓▓▓▓▓▓▓▓▓▓▓▓▓▓▓▓▓▓▓▓▓▓▓▓▓▓▓▓▓▓▓▓▓▓

1 BRITAIN GAZETTEER Information on over
  a thousand towns in Britain.Tourist
  notes for all towns,travel,transport,
  accommodation,restaurants,events,
  & entertainment for larger towns.
  Information supplied by the British
  Tourist Authority,alphabetic index by
  town name
2 TOWNS IN ENGLAND The same info as in
  choice 1,but indexed by region &
  county
3 TOWNS IN SCOTLAND The same info as in
  choice 1,but indexed by region
4 TOWNS IN WALES The same info as in
  choice 1,but indexed by county


▓▓▓▓▓▓▓▓▓▓▓▓▓▓▓▓▓▓▓▓▓▓▓▓▓▓▓▓▓▓▓▓▓▓▓▓▓▓▓▓
```

Towns in England

||||||||||||||||||||||||||||||||||||||||||||||||||||||||||||||||||||||||||

1 GREATER LONDON
2 SOUTH EAST Kent,Sussex,Surrey,Hants,
  Berks,Oxon,Bucks,Bedford,Herts,Essex,
  Isle of Wight.
3 SOUTH WEST Cornwall,Devon,Somerset,
  Dorset,Wiltshire,Avon,Gloucestershire
4 EAST ANGLIA Norfolk,Suffolk,Cambridge
5 EAST MIDLANDS Derby,Nottingham,Lincs,
  Northampton,Leicester.
6 WEST MIDLANDS Warwick,Hereford,Worcs,
  Shropshire,Staffs,West Midlands
7 NORTH WEST Lancs.,Cheshire,Merseyside
  Greater Manchester
8 YORKSHIRE/HUMBER Humberside,North,
  South & West Yorkshire.
9 NORTH Tyne & Wear,Cleveland,Durham,
  Northumberland,Cumbria
0 BRITAIN INDEX ||||||||||||||||||||||||||||||||||||

South West Region - England

||||||||||||||||||||||||||||||||||||||||||||||||||||||||||||||||||||||||||

Information on a number of towns in
each county:

1 AVON 9 towns
2 CORNWALL 34 towns
3 DEVON 36 towns
4 DORSET 15 towns
5 GLOUCESTERSHIRE 14 towns
6 SOMERSET 18 towns
7 WILTSHIRE 16 towns
8 ISLES OF SCILLY

0 REGIONS OF ENGLAND INDEX
||||||||||||||||||||||||||||||||||||||||||||||||||||||||||||||||||||||||||

Avon

▓▓

10 BATH
11 BRISTOL
12 CLEVEDON

20 MIDSOMER NORTON
21 PORTISHEAD
22 WESTON-SUPER-MARE
23 YATTON

0 SOUTH WEST ENGLAND INDEX

▓▓

BTA 220   220614a   Op

Bristol

Avon   Population 411,800

0 Tourist notes
1 Travel and Transport
2 Accommodation and Restaurants
3 Activities/Entertainments/Events
4 Local Businesses
6 Education and Training
7 Local and Community Information
Information will be added as available
under: Other Information

▓▓

Market Fri,Sat   Early closing Wed,Sat
City just off the M4, 88 miles south
west of Birmingham, 113 miles west of
London. Cardiff 44 miles, Exeter 75.
Railway station provides 125 High Speed
Train services to London.
                    GAZETTEER INDEX....9

Bristol is one example of only 122 'major' towns at this stage, ie those with significant amounts of data linked to them. In addition to those, there are about 800 towns with minimal detail waiting for the demand for information to be annexed on to them. One example is Broadway, where the town page routes at present lead only to Dormy House, one of our commended establishments.

```
BTA 220                    2206134Sa        Op
   BROADWAY  Hereford & Worcester
Pop 3,000                  Early closing Thur

Village 15m S of Stratford-upon-Avon on
A44. Cheltenham 15m  London 92m
Nearest station Moreton-in-Marsh 9m
Lovely village situated at the foot of
the Cotswolds. Many interesting old
houses,some dating back to Elizabethan
times. Attractive village green and
plenty of old pubs and inns.
Special features
#  14c Abbots Grange and Priors Manse
#  Buckland Rectory 1m SW
#  Snowshill Manor 3m SE

DORMY HOUSE British Tourist Authority
Commended Hotel.....................1
LYGON ARMS British Tourist Authority
Commended Hotel.................... 2

              GAZETTEER INDEX...9
```

```
BTA 220                     220263a        Op
         BTA COMMENDED HOTEL 1982
```

*** AA   *** RAC

DORMY HOUSE
BROADWAY,
WORCESTERSHIRE

```
Unique hotel with marvellous views,high
in the hills over Broadway.Excellent
food & wine,beautiful bedrooms & public
areas created from original sixteenth
century building. 50 bedrooms,all with
private bath,direct dial phone,colour
TV.Excellent conference facilities.
Bookable through travel agents
--Telephone 0386 852711 Telex 338571---
TARIFF..# CONFERENCES..1 INDEX..2
    BTA GAZETTEER OF BRITAIN........9
```

I hope all this has demonstrated the enormous scope for development in the project, and the value it should have for the Prestel user. We expect to have about 2000 - 3000 towns in two years from now. On our computer database, we have about 6000 towns, and clearly there are many more towns than that in Britain. Equally clearly, there is no point in creating a massive index which leads to no information, and therefore the gazetteer will be demand-driven.

The issues raised by the project are quite important ones, such as the need for control on standards, both of the tourist product and of the presentation of information; the prospect of 'direct sell' of travel, ie the consumer buying direct without the intervention (and commission) of the agent; the need for cooperation among information providers to promote use of the overall service.

Going from there, as Ric Foot mentioned, we intend to start in 1983 the development of a BRITAIN database, incorporating BTA, British Council and the Central Office of Information, for the reasons mentioned earlier. This does not exist yet, of course, but the principle can be demonstrated in outline, based on what you have already seen. The main entry pages look like this:

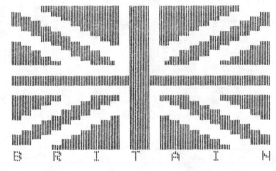

GAZETTEER OF BRITAIN

Gazetteer

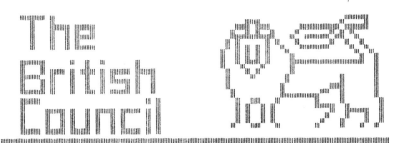

Information & cross-
references to many
towns in Great
Britain, the Channel
Islands & Isle of Man.

Alphabetical town index:
1 A, B
2 C, D, E, F, G
3 H, I, J, K, L
4 M, N, O, P, Q, R
5 S, T, U, V, W, X, Y, Z

6 Channel Islands
7 Isle of Man

9 Regional index
    BTA MAIN INDEX...0   IPs......key 8

British Council (c 1982)

The British Council

Key 0 from any frame to return here

CONTENTS
1 Short courses viewdatabase
2 To contact the British Council
More about the British Council

    Key 9 for British Tourist Authority,
    0 for Prestel main index

WELCOME TO B T A ON PRESTEL
THE BRITISH TOURIST AUTHORITY
These pages contain a range of
information on tourism and
tourist facilities.
1 MAIN INDEX
2 ABOUT BTA 3 SEND US A MESSAGE
4 BTA'S VIEWDATA SERVICES

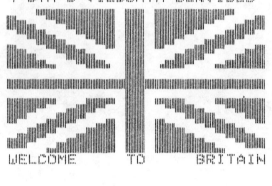

WELCOME   TO   BRITAIN

Government Information 5001a   0p
COI

GUIDE TO Government Services

1 INDEXES TO GOVERNMENT INFORMATION
  ON PRESTEL

2 GOVERNMENT DEPARTMENTS What they do,
  their responsibilities and who to
  contact.
3 GOVERNMENT MINISTERS The Cabinet,
  Departmental Ministers, Officers of
  the Queen's Household and Government
  Whips.
4 PRESS RELEASES Agriculture; Industry
  and Trade; Health & Safety at Work;
  Statistics.
5 INITIALS INDEX What those government
  initials mean!

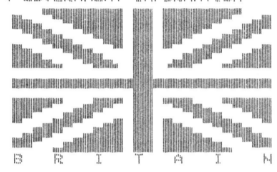

WELCOME TO BRITAIN ON PRESTEL
The BRITAIN database presents a
wide range of information for the
home and overseas user.

    1 GAZETTEER OF BRITAIN
    2 BRITISH COUNCIL
    3 BRITISH TOURIST AUTHORITY
    4 GOVERNMENT INFORMATION

B   R   I   T   A   I   N

So those are the main components of what will become the
BRITAIN database. There are some major issues arising from this
as well, which we have already begun to tackle.

The geographical index is, of course, a major information
tool of benefit to all users, but perhaps more significant is the
complementary need for good subject (or in our case, product)
indexing. BTA has just finished building a thesaurus of tourism
terms - over 2000 terms - to serve as a controlled vocabulary for
indexing purposes, possibly keyword indexing which system operators
like British Telecom are keen to pursue.

We suspect that probably our subject indexing will be produced
on paper, to serve as a complement to the viewdata system and to
assist rapid identification of the desired information. Taking into
account that ours will be developed into a multi-lingual thesaurus
for overseas users, it is even more likely to be a printed index
rather than one which is built into the system. However, there may
be scope for other formulae.

This leads also to the issue of overseas dissemination. As
part of the BRITAIN database project, BTA and the British Council
will be placing Prestel sets in selected overseas offices; the
objective will be to test the usefulness of viewdata as a mechanism
for disseminating this kind of information, but also, we hope, to
act as a catalyst with the overseas national systems on which we are
already represented, to explore how far we can realistically use

Prestel as a world viewdata service, which is how it is promoted, as opposed to using the overseas national viewdata systems, possibly back-to-back with Prestel. There is clearly a case for being represented on those overseas systems, but at what point you transfer from that into Prestel, and how the Gateway mechanisms work is being hotly debated among PTT's and probably won't be resolved until some information providers actually create the need for it to be resolved.

In thirty minutes, I have only been able to describe these projects in outline. Complex information services require sophisticated systems and technology to deliver them, but don't let us forget that what the customer wants is both specific and simple, and if he fails to be well served in those respects, no amount of information technology will ever take off. That is why we must ensure the contribution of the skills of those who are professionally trained and experienced in the information business.

APPENDIX 1

Authors' Biographical Notes

DAVID BARR
After an early career in academic librarian-
ship at Warwick University and Hatfield Polytechnic, David Barr worked in Information
Publishing with Xerox Publishing Group, prior
to his present appointment, which commenced in
1978, as Manager of Information Services at the
British Tourist Authority.

He is the author of several papers on academic/
management literature and founding Editor/Publisher
of 'Management Research News'.

DAVID BIRD
From Birmingham University, David Bird worked
for ICL in a variety of jobs, in both a technical
and sales capacity. He joined the Great Universal
Stores group in 1967 and took responsibility for
designing the shape and structure of GUS computing.

PAUL BRADLEY
Paul Bradley is an industrial marketing specialist
who has been with Philips for the past fourteen
years, the past five concentrating on LaserVision.

JOHN BUTCHER
Appointed Parliamentary Under Secretary of State
for Industry in April 1982, Mr Butcher has been
MP for Coventry South West since May 1979.

Since 1968 he has been an executive in the computer
industry with special experience of microcomputers
and microelectronics.

He has served as Vice-Chairman of the All-Party
Information Technology Committee and as Secretary
of the Conservative Parliamentary Industry Committee.

Born in 1946, he was educated at Huntingdon Grammar
School, Birmingham University and the Institute of
Strategic Studies in London.

RIC FOOT
Ric Foot joined Philips in 1954 as a Management
Trainee after an Honours degree in Classics at
Worcester College, Oxford.

His subsequent career was in the lighting field,
ultimately being appointed Divisional Director of
the Lighting Division in 1976. He was also a
Director of the Lighting Industry Federation at
this time. He took over responsibility for
Philips Video Division at the end of 1977.

Early in 1981, he was seconded to the Department of Industry to assist with the market development of teletext and for this work, he was elected 'Electrical Industry - Personality of the Year'. In addition to maintaining the teletext initiatives, he is currently engaged in similar work for the UK market development of viewdata.

FRANK E HALL

Frank Hall was formerly Financial Director of British Relay and is a member of Council and also a member of the Cable Television Association of GB since 1958 (Chairman 1966 and 1980); National Television Rental Association since 1958 (Chairman 1968, 1969 & 1975).

GEOFF HUTT

Geoff Hutt is responsible for the development of Viewdata including the Dealer Network communications interface at BLSL. Before taking up this role, he worked for several years within the systems function of BL, concentrating on production and material control aspects.

PAT MONTAGUE

Pat Montague was Assistant Production Manager at the Manchester Evening News from 1965-71 and subsequently Assistant to the Managing Director at Lancashire Colour Printers.

In 1972, he joined the Birmingham Post and Mail as Director/General Manager. In 1977, he also became Director in Charge of Viewtel. His other interests include the Videotex Industry Association of which he is Deputy Chairman.

JOHN RADCLIFFE

John Radcliffe is the Executive Producer responsible for the highly successful BBC Computer Literacy Project.

DAVID WILSON

After a Cambridge degree in Maths and Physics, David Wilson decided to become a journalist. He worked on various provincial papers and in BBC News, Birmingham, before coming to BBC News in London in 1960, becoming their Science Correspondent in 1963.

He was appointed to the newly-created post of Manager, Teletext at the beginning of November 1982.

APPENDIX 2

Seminar Organisation

Committee:

G P Andrew FBIM ALA
formerly of Royal Borough of Kingston
upon Thames Library Service
R Foot MA
Department of Industry
D F W Hawes MA FRSA FLA
Polytechnic of the South Bank Library Service
R G Lester BSc PhD ARIC MIInfSc
London Business School
C Smith BSc MIInfSc
Technical Change Centre

Administration:

R E Palmer, Library Association
G M Shipway, Library Association

Audio Visual:

B Openshaw
Polytechnic of the South Bank

The Committee wish to express their thanks to John Beishon BSc DPhil CEng MIM, Director of the Polytechnic of the South Bank for allowing the Seminar to be held there and for making the Polytechnic resources and facilities so freely available; and also to the members of Library staff for their enthusiastic assistance.

Typed and produced by Gillian M Shipway BA MA